PAW PATROL™: ANNUAL 2019
A CENTUM BOOK 9781912564965
Published in Great Britain by Centum Books Ltd
This edition published 2018
1 3 5 7 9 10 8 6 4 2

© 2018 Spin Master PAW Productions Inc. All Rights Reserved. PAW Patrol and all related titles, logos and characters are trademarks of Spin Master Ltd. Nickelodeon and all related titles and logos are trademarks of Viacom International Inc.
All rights reserved. No part of this publication may be reproduced, stored in a retrieval system, or transmitted in any form or by any means, electronic, mechanical, photocopying, recording or otherwise, without the prior permission of the publishers.
Centum Books Ltd, 20 Devon Square, Newton Abbot, Devon, TQ12 2HR, UK
books@centumbooksltd.co.uk
CENTUM BOOKS Limited Reg. No. 07641486
A CIP catalogue record for this book is available from the British Library
Printed in Italy

ANNUAL 2019

centum

Contents

- 7 Welcome to Adventure Bay
- 8 Get to know the pups - Chase
- 9 My nose knows!
- 10 Pup, pup and away
- 12 To the Lookout
- 14 Get to know the pups - Marshall
- 15 Ready for a ruff, ruff rescue
- 16 Playful colouring
- 17 Dot-to-spot
- 18 Story: Mission PAW
- 26 Recall to action
- 28 Get to know the pups - Rubble
- 29 Rubble on the double
- 30 Pup patterns
- 31 Time for treats
- 32 Counting on you
- 33 Home sweet home
- 34 Get to know the pups - Skye
- 35 This pup's gotta fly!
- 36 The PAW Patrol is on the job!
- 38 It's a jungle out there!
- 40 Get to know the pups - Rocky
- 41 Ready, steady, Rocky!
- 42 Colouring code: TEAMWORK
- 44 Yelp for help!
- 46 Get to know the pups - Zuma
- 47 Let's dive in!
- 48 Posters
- 50 Get to know the pups - Tracker
- 51 Jungle rescue
- 52 Story: Meet Tracker
- 60 Get to know the pups - Everest
- 61 Play in the snow
- 62 All the apples
- 64 Pups at play
- 66 Ready for action activities
- 68 Fire training trail
- 70 Cone crazy
- 71 Back in the box
- 72 PAWsome masks
- 73 Doggy dominoes
- 74 Answers

Get to know the pups

Chase

Chase is a top police dog. His Pup Pack opens to give him a megaphone, a searchlight, and a net that shoots out to catch things.

Net shoots out here

Pup Pack

Megaphone

Name: Chase
Breed: German Shepherd
Skills: Herding traffic, blocking off dangerous roads and solving mysteries.

Did you know?
Chase can sniff out anything, but he happens to be allergic to both cats and feathers!

8

My nose knows!

Chase needs to get to the Lookout. Help guide him through the streets of Adventure Bay, avoiding the kittens.

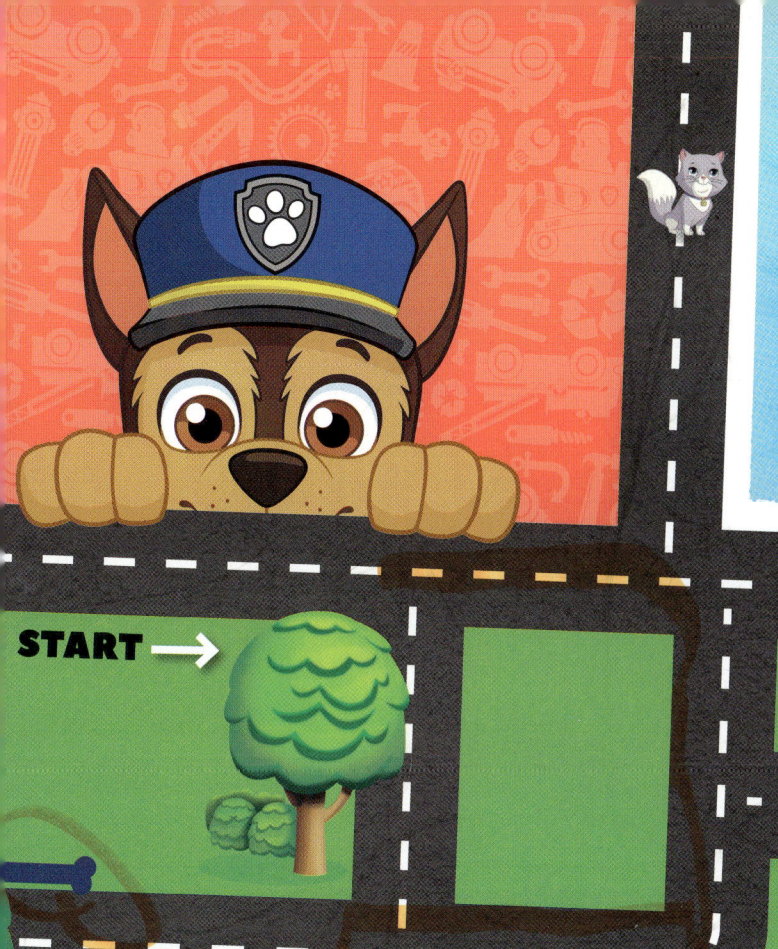

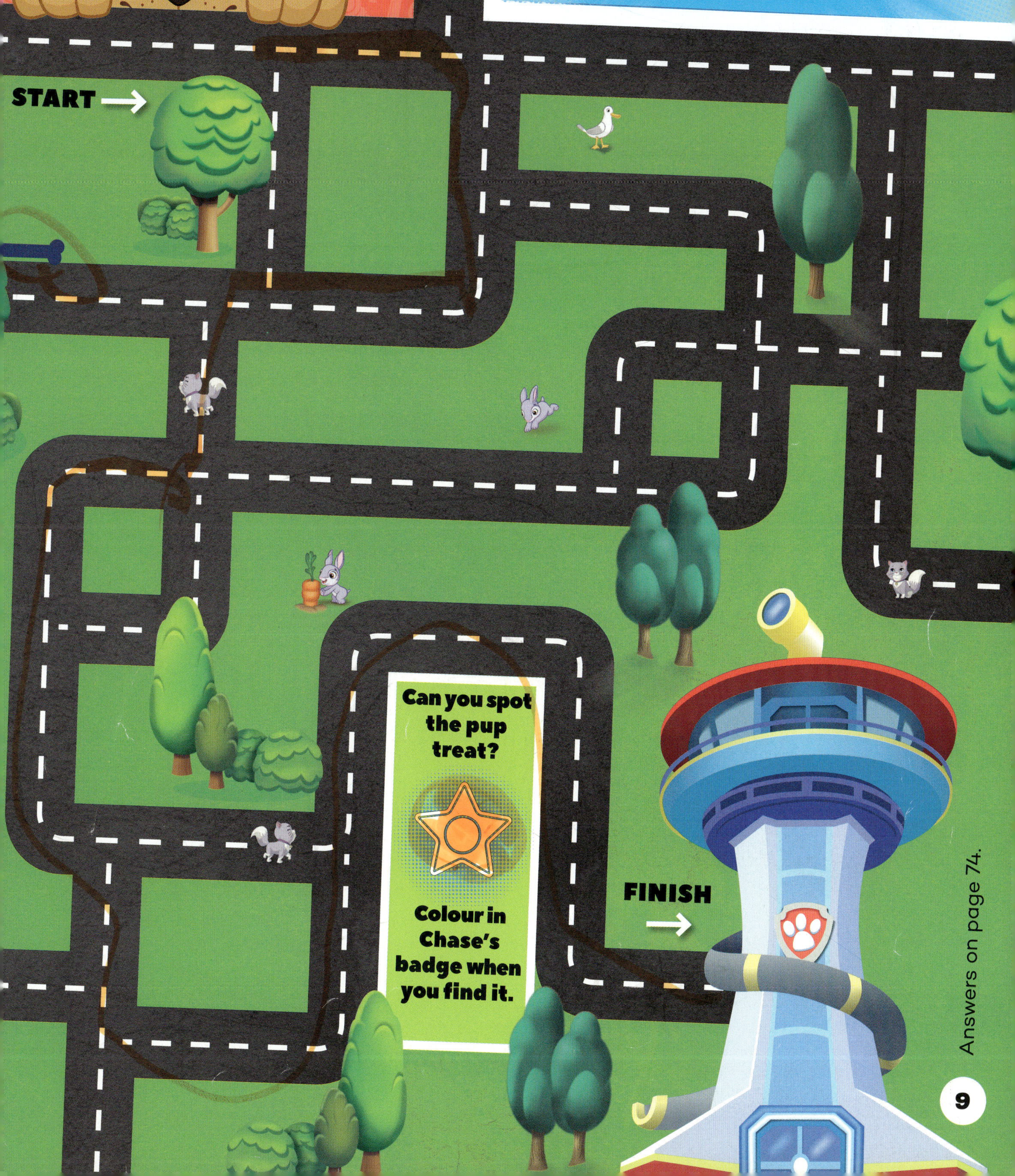

Answers on page 74.

To the Lookout

The pups have lost some of their favourite things. Can you spot all of the items in the big picture? Tick each one when you find it.

Get to know the pups

Marshall

Marshall is a brave fire dog. His Pup Pack contains an amazing fire hose with two water jets.

Double-spray fire hose

Pup Pack

Name: Marshall
Breed: Dalmatian
Skills: Can smell and detect gas leaks and smoke, and is really fast at running.

Did you know?
He gets too excited and can be a little clumsy!

Ready for a ruff, ruff rescue

Design an obstacle course so Marshall can practise his fire-rescue skills.

Why not add some rubble for Marshall to get past?

Did someone say 'Rubble'?

Add some cones for Marshall to go around.

Can you spot the pup treat?

Colour in Marshall's badge when you find it.

You could draw some wooden obstacles for Marshall to jump over.

15

Dot-to-spot

Marshall is an amazing fire-rescue pup. Join the dots to complete the picture, then colour in the PAWsome rescue pup!

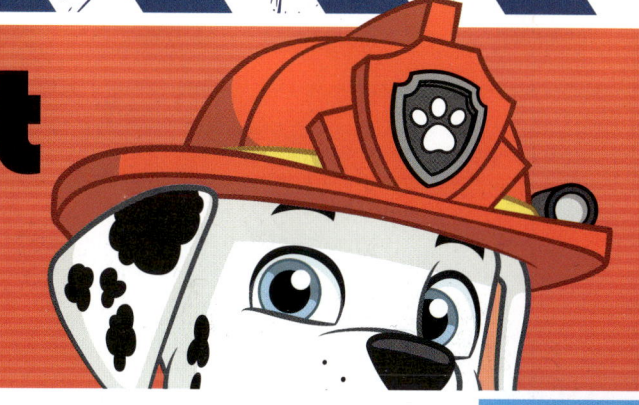

I'm fired up!

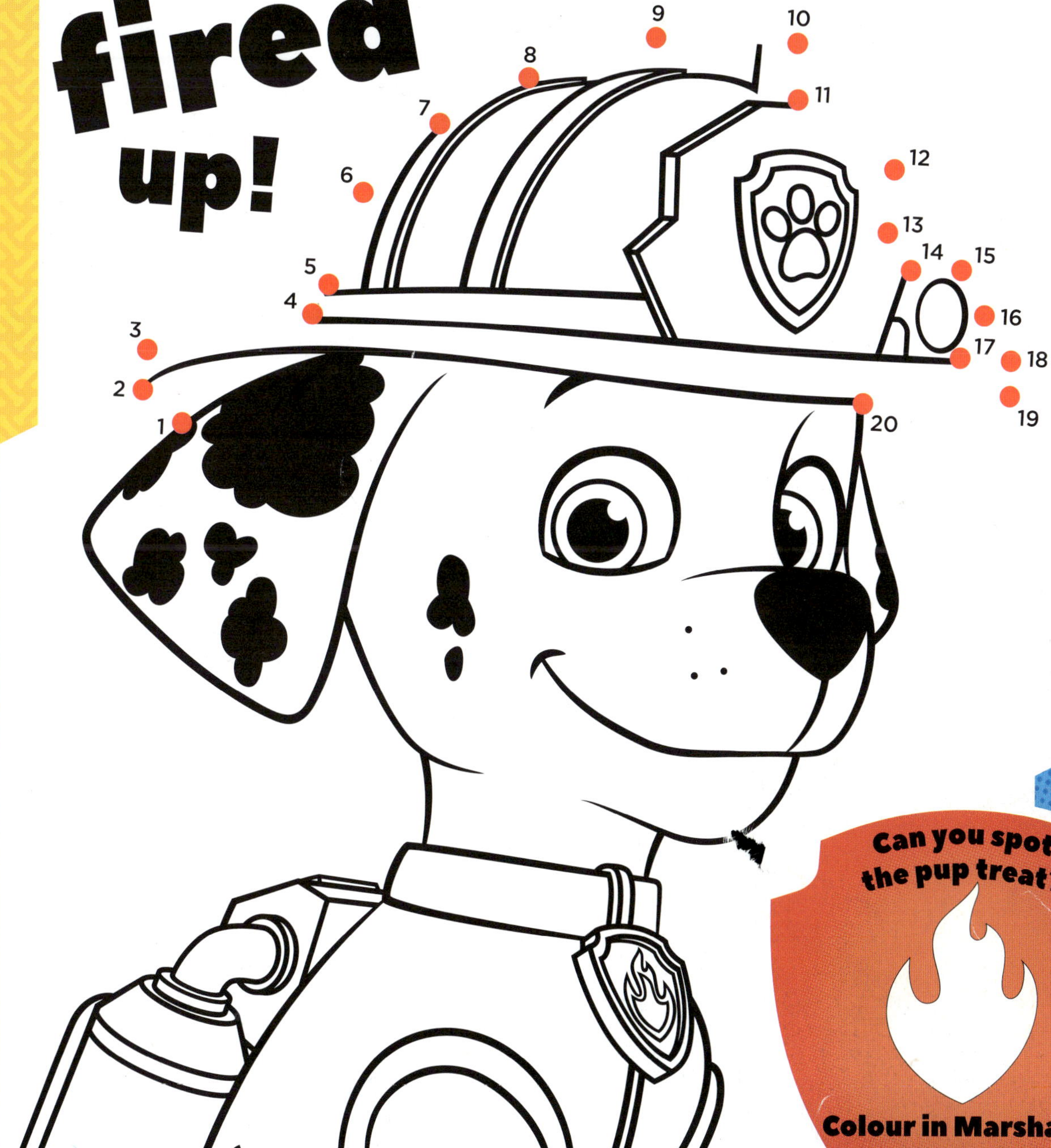
1
2
3
4
5
6
7
8
9
10
11
12
13
14
15
16
17
18
19
20

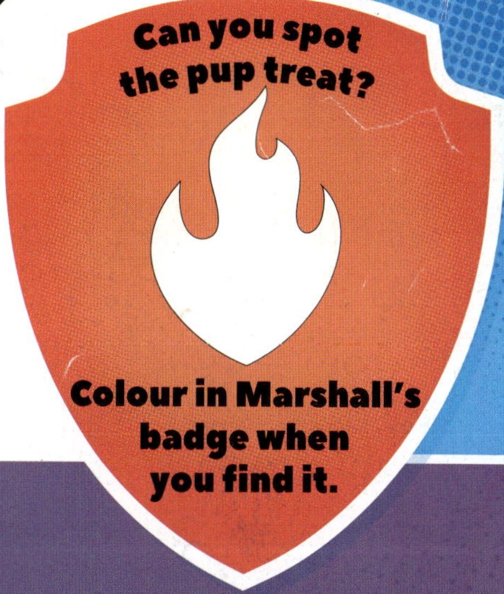
Can you spot the pup treat?
Colour in Marshall's badge when you find it.

Answers on page 74.

Mission PAW

Chase was on his way to an important mission in the city of Barkingburg, to guard the royal crown. He arrived on the Air Patroller and flew down to Barkingburg Castle.

The streets of the city were quiet. Nobody noticed the PAW Patrol hero gliding down to the castle rooftop. Chase was on the case!

Chase quickly changed into his smartest outfit, with a special Pup Tag bow tie. Then he met the Princess of Barkingburg, her uncle the Earl and her pup Sweetie.
"I'm so glad you could help us," said the Princess.

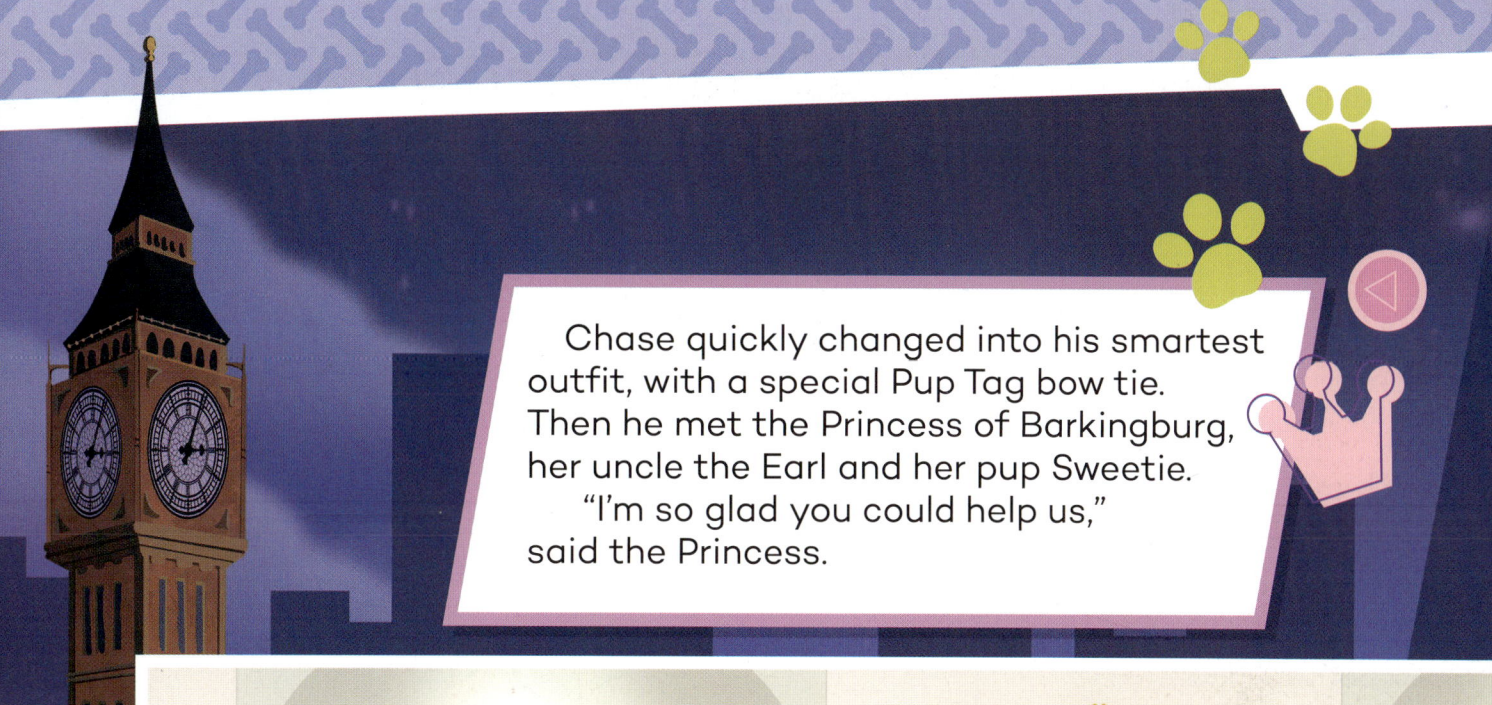

"I like your bow tie," said Sweetie and smiled at Chase. "Thanks," said Chase. "It helps me stay in contact with Ryder." He didn't mention the camera hidden inside it. That was his superspy secret!

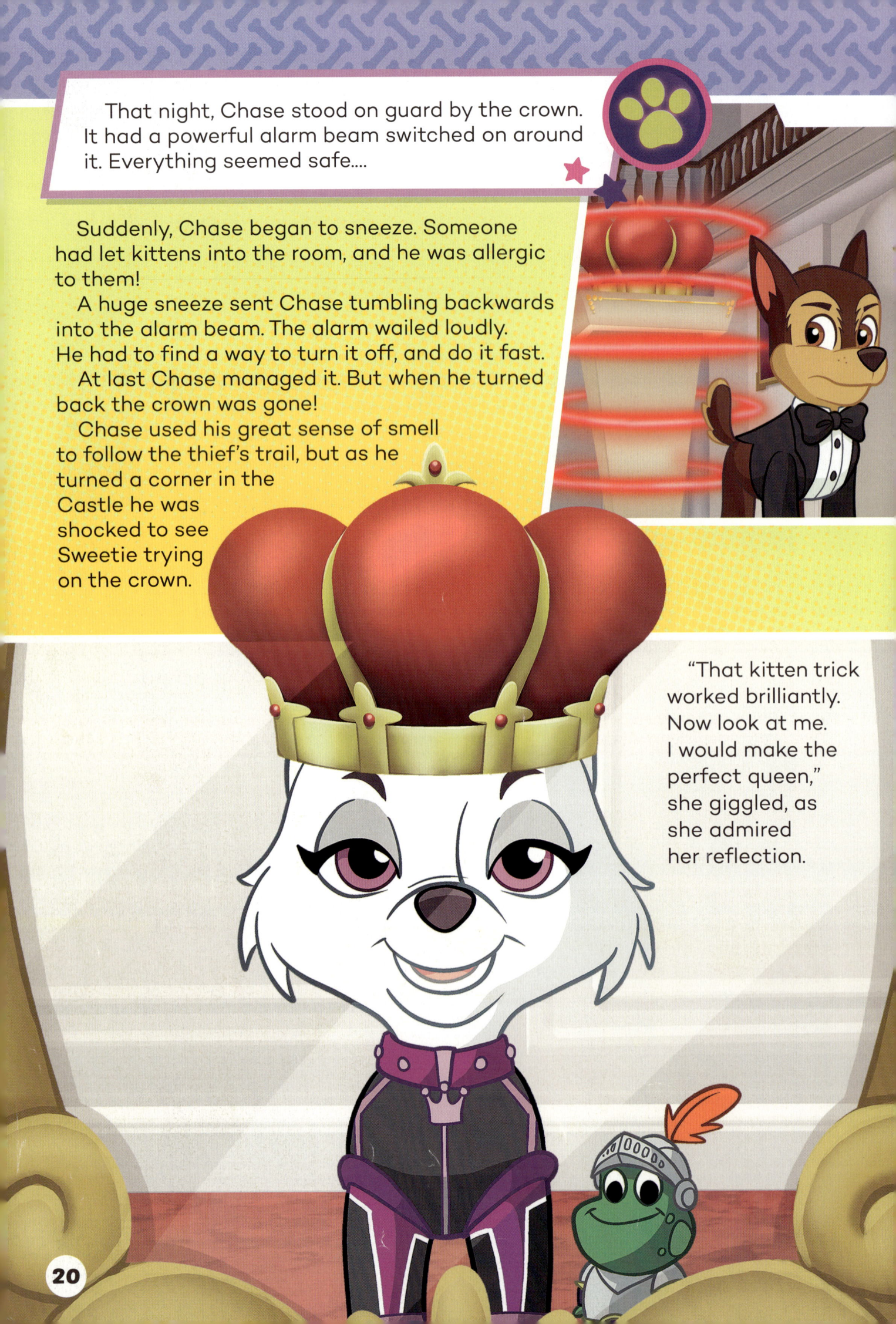

That night, Chase stood on guard by the crown. It had a powerful alarm beam switched on around it. Everything seemed safe....

Suddenly, Chase began to sneeze. Someone had let kittens into the room, and he was allergic to them!

A huge sneeze sent Chase tumbling backwards into the alarm beam. The alarm wailed loudly. He had to find a way to turn it off, and do it fast.

At last Chase managed it. But when he turned back the crown was gone!

Chase used his great sense of smell to follow the thief's trail, but as he turned a corner in the Castle he was shocked to see Sweetie trying on the crown.

"That kitten trick worked brilliantly. Now look at me. I would make the perfect queen," she giggled, as she admired her reflection.

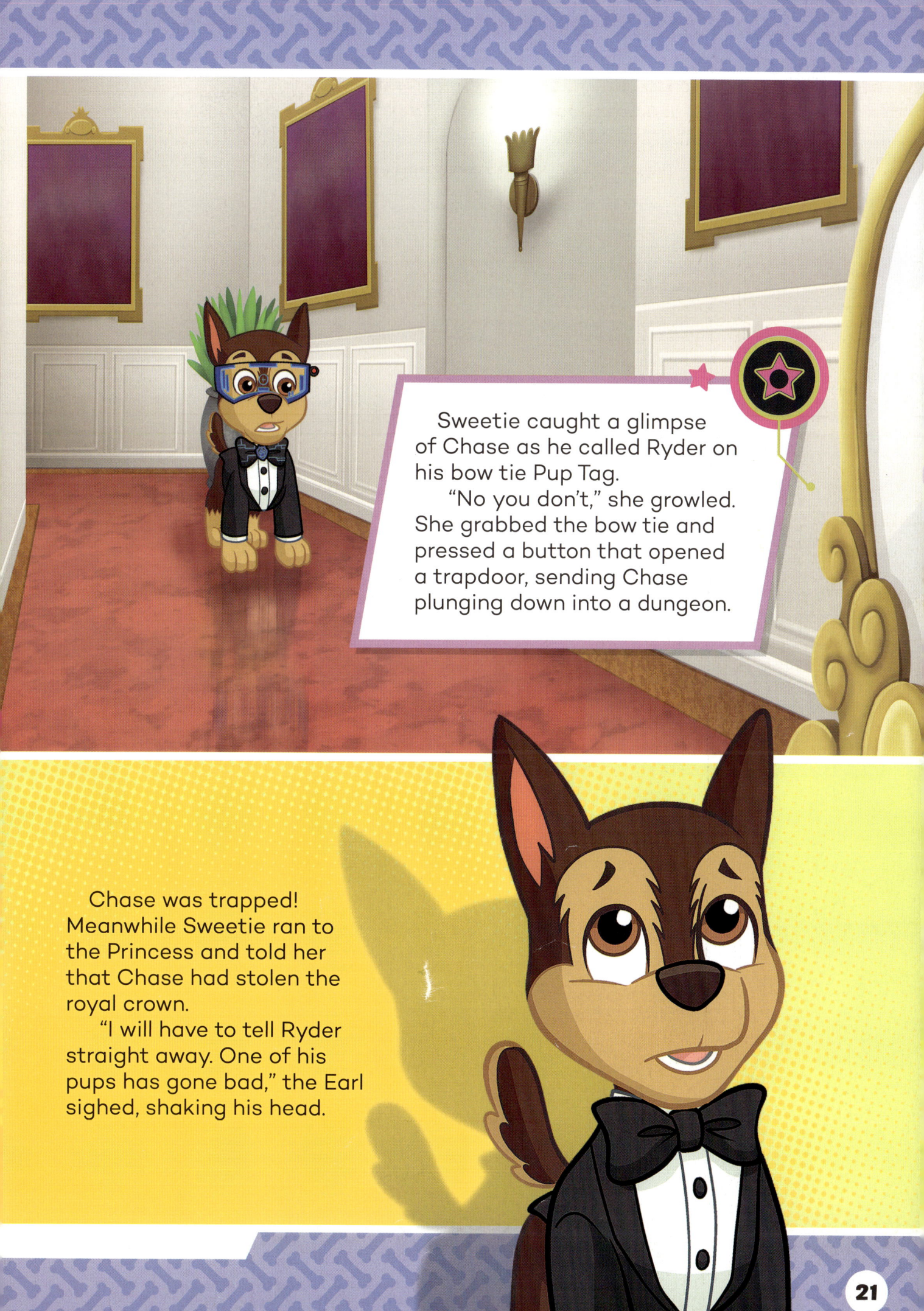

When Ryder got the call, he didn't believe for one moment that Chase was guilty.

"Chase needs help," he said. "Come on PAW Patrol. It's Mission PAW time!"

The Air Patroller got the PAW Patrol to Barkingburg fast, and they were soon ready for action using their all-new Mission PAW equipment.

Sweetie had thrown the bow tie into the castle moat. Zuma dived into the water in his Aqua Drone, using sonar to locate the bow tie's signal.

Chase heard his friend through the wall of his dungeon and used his tennis ball cannon to fire balls at the wall.

Bang! Bang!

"What's that?" cried Zuma, hearing the thuds through his sonar. The banging noise helped Ryder and the pups locate Chase in the dungeon.

Now it was Rubble's turn to help.
"Rubble on the double!" he called and turned on his amazing Mini Miner. *Whirrrrrrrr.*

The Mini Miner was perfect for breaking through the wall of the castle to get to Chase's dungeon.

"Am I glad to see you!" cried Chase. He quickly told his friends what Sweetie had done. "My bow tie camera filmed everything," he explained.

Recall to action

The PAW Patrol has just completed another successful mission in Adventure Bay. Look at this picture for 30 seconds. Then cover the bottom half of these pages with paper and try to answer the questions. If you like, you can write your answers on the paper.

Can you spot the pup treat?

Colour in Chase's badge when you find it.

1. Which pup is licking Ryder's cheek?

chase

2. Are Skye's goggles blue or pink?

PINK

3. Which pup is wearing a red Pup Pack?

4. What is Zuma carrying in his mouth?

5. Is Everest next to Marshall or next to Skye?

6. Is Rubble wearing his yellow helmet?

Answers on page 74.

Rubble

Rubble is a tough construction dog. His Pup Pack opens to reveal a bucket arm scoop for digging and lifting large and heavy objects.

Name: Rubble
Breed: Bulldog
Skills: Superior digging and construction skills, plus he's an excellent skate and snow boarder.

Did you know?
He doesn't like spiders or being in deep water.

Get to know the pups

Bucket scoop

Rubble on the double

Rubble loves to dig. Can you spot the picture of this ruff, tough pup below that is different from the rest?

a

b

Can you spot the pup treat?

Colour in Chase's badge when you find it.

c

d

Answers on page 74.

Pup patterns

Complete the patterns by working out which picture comes next in each row. Use the key below and write the letter of the correct picture in each empty shield.

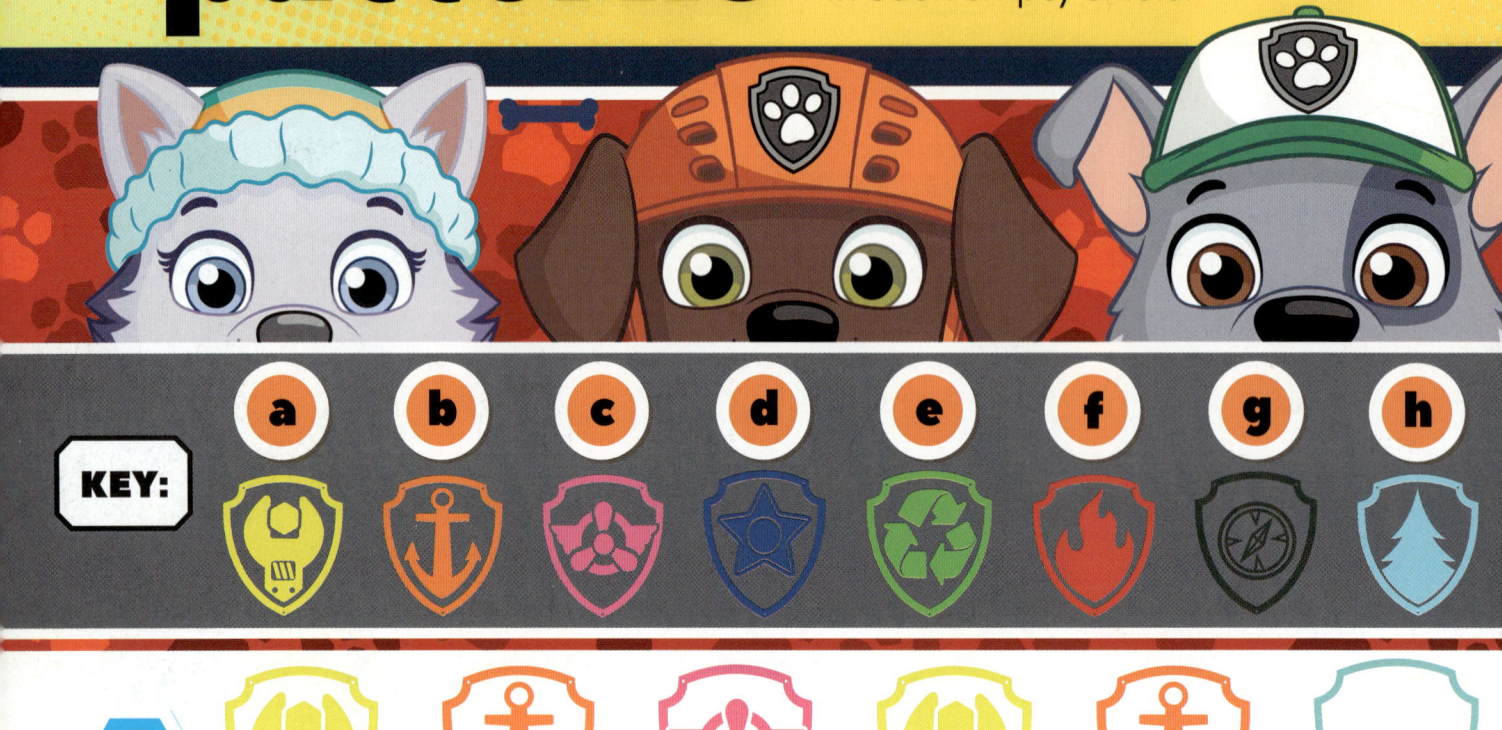

KEY:
a, b, c, d, e, f, g, h

1.

2.

3.

4.

Can you spot the pup treat?  **Colour in Chase's badge when you find it.**

30 Answers on page 74.

Time for treats

Help Marshall find the bowl of tasty treats. He can only step on the paw prints in the order shown below. He can move forwards, backwards up and down.

FOLLOW THIS ORDER

START

Can you spot the pup treat?  **Colour in Chase's badge when you find it.**

Answers on page 74.

Counting on you

If you're in trouble, you can rely on the PAW Patrol to help out!
Look at this page, then use your number skills to count up the pup pictures.

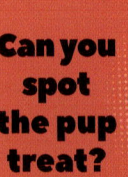

Can you spot the pup treat? Colour in Chase's badge when you find it.

1 Marshall
Circle the right number:
1 2 3 4 5 6 7 8 9 10

2 Skye
Circle the right number:
1 2 3 4 5 6 7 8 9 10

3 Zuma
Circle the right number:
1 2 3 4 5 6 7 8 9 10

4 Rocky
Circle the right number:
1 2 3 4 5 6 7 8 9 10

Answers on page 74.

Home sweet home

Ryder and the PAW Patrol love their Lookout in Adventure Bay! Draw lines to link the missing pieces to the correct place in the picture.

Can you spot the pup treat? Colour in Skye's badge when you find it.

Answers on page 75.

33

Get to know the pups

Skye

Skye is a pilot dog. Her Pup Pack opens to reveal wings that allow her to fly.

Flying goggles

Wings

Pup Pack

Name: Skye
Breed: Cockapoo
Skills: High-flying rescues! She is a fearless daredevil who will try anything with a smile.

Did you know?
Skye loves playing her favourite video game, *Pup Pup Boogie*.

Can you spot the pup treat?

Colour in Skye's badge when you find it.

This pup's gotta fly!

Skye has been busy flying over Adventure Bay and taking pictures. Draw a line to match up each photograph with the correct location.

a. The Pup Park

b. The PAW Patrol Lookout

c. Seal Island

d. Farmer Yumi's Farm

e. The train station

Answers on page 75.

35

The PAW Patrol is on the job!

The PAW Patrol is lined up and ready for action! As soon as a call comes in, it's all paws on deck. Take a look at the pup pictures, then answer the questions.

Who is the tallest member of the team?

Who is the smallest member of the team?

Which pups are wearing green hats?

Which pups are wearing helmets?

Which pup has got a woolly hat on?

Which pup is wearing a police hat?

Can you spot the pup treat?

Colour in Skye's badge when you find it.

Answers on page 75.

It's a jungle out there!

Get ready to go jungle tracking with the PAW Patrol. Each picture in the panel along the bottom appears somewhere in the big picture. Can you find them all?

Can you spot the pup treat?

Colour in Tracker's badge when you find it.

Can you spot these, too?

Answers on page 75.

39

Rocky

Rocky is a creative recycling pup. His Pup Pack contains a mechanical claw, as well as tools like a screwdriver and ratchet.

Get to know the pups

Mechanical claw

Tools in pack

Screwdriver

Name: Rocky
Breed: Mixed breed
Skills: Reducing, reusing and recycling anything he can find.

Did you know?
Rocky is not a fan of baths and doesn't like getting wet at all.

40

Ready, steady, Rocky!

Help Rocky complete these picture patterns. Point to the object that comes next in each row, and then write the correct letter in the circle.

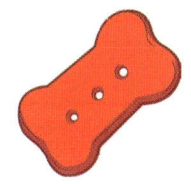

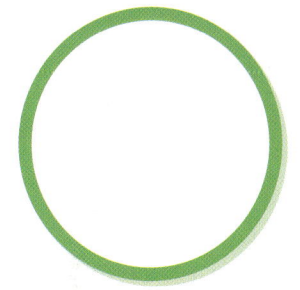

1) gloves, bone, gloves, gloves, ◯

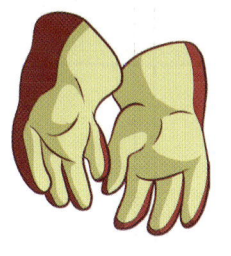

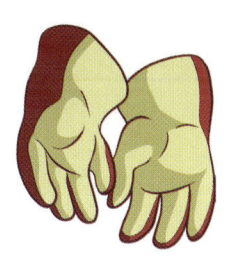

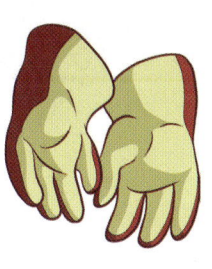

2) bowl, bone, bowl, bone, ◯

3) cap, cap, gloves, cap, ◯

Can you spot the pup treat?
Colour in Rocky's badge when you find it. 

- **a** gloves
- **b** cap
- **c** bone
- **d** bowl

Answers on page 75.   41

Colouring code: TEAMWORK

The PAW Patrol has its very own superpower, TEAMWORK! Colour the picture using the colour key below. There is a guide at the top of the opposite page to help you.

Wow!

1 — yellow
2 — orange
3 — red
4 — green

Can you spot the pup treat?

Colour in Rocky's badge when you find it.

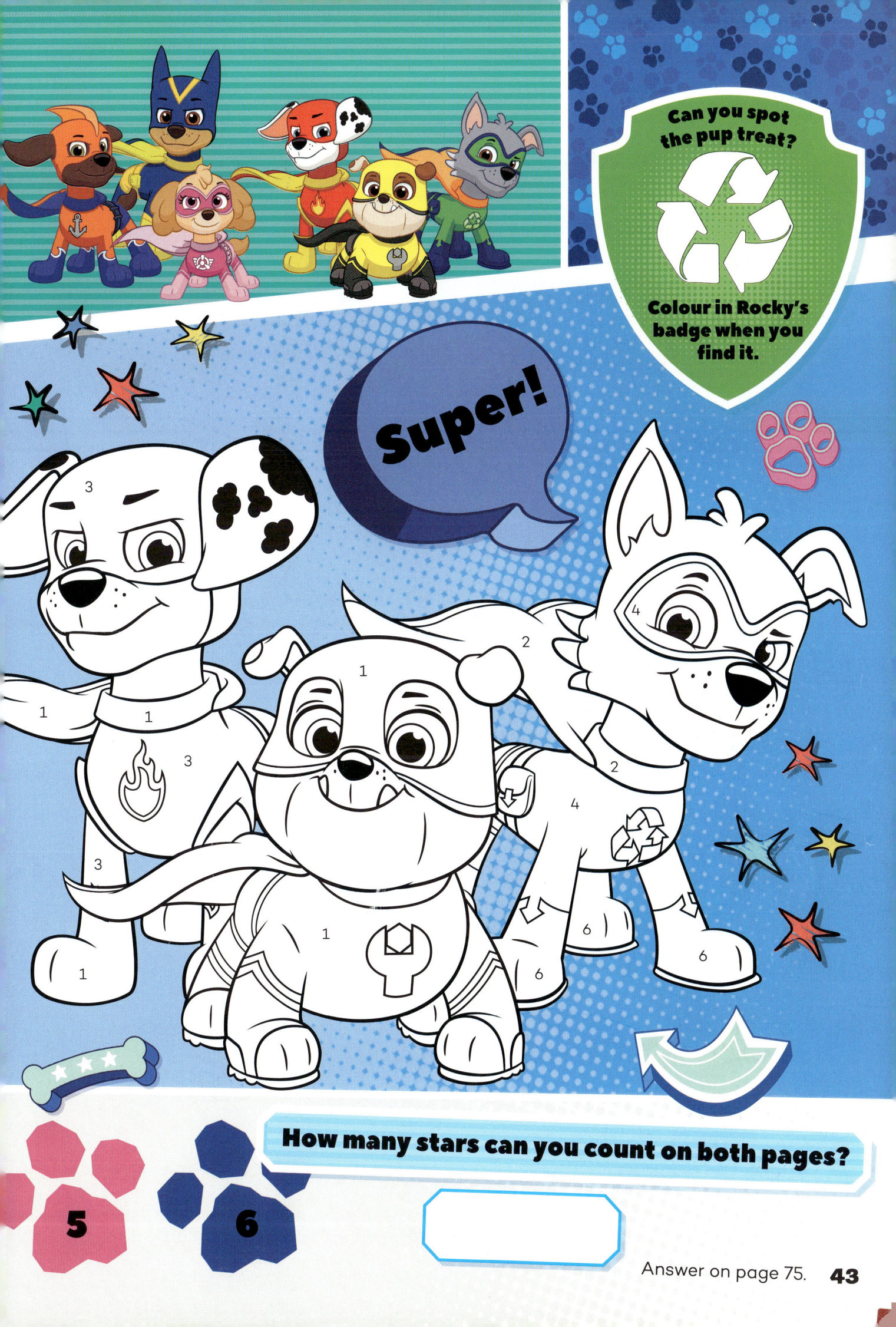

Super!

How many stars can you count on both pages?

Answer on page 75.

Yelp for help!

Uh oh! The name of each pup has been mixed up. Write the correct name below the jumbled up version, then draw a line to the correct pup on the opposite page.

1. CSAHE

2. MRAASHLL

3. RCKOY

4. YKSE

5. ZMAU

6. RBULBE

7. RACTKER

8. RESTEVE

Can you spot the pup treat?

Colour in Zuma's badge when you find it.

Answers on page 75.

45

Zuma

Zuma is the team's water rescue dog. His Pup Pack contains air tanks and propellers so he can dive and swim deep underwater.

Name: Zuma
Breed: Labrador
Skills: Excellent at swimming and diving.

Did you know?
Zuma has lots of energy for any adventure in store for him!

Air tanks

Get to know the pups

Let's dive in!

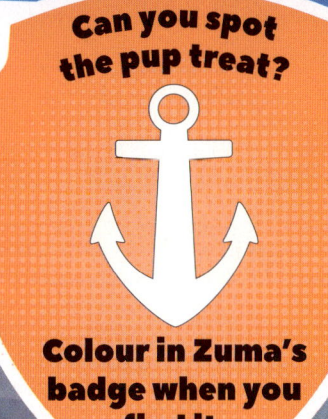

Can you spot the pup treat?

Colour in Zuma's badge when you find it.

It's time for an underwater adventure! Can you help Zuma count the fish?

1 How many  can you count?

2 How many can you count?

3 How many can you count?

Answers on page 75.

Scuba Pups

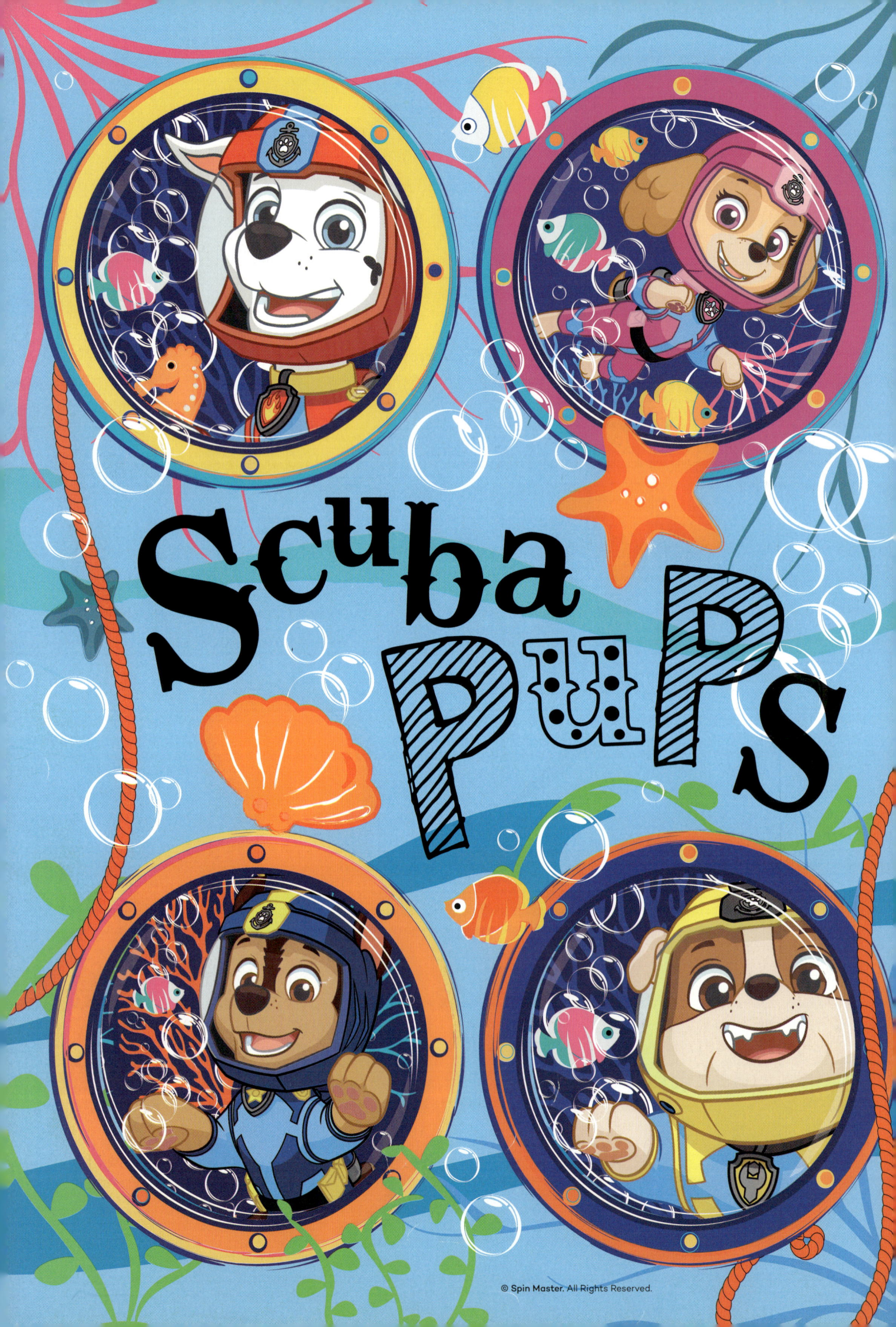

NEVER STOP *dreaming*

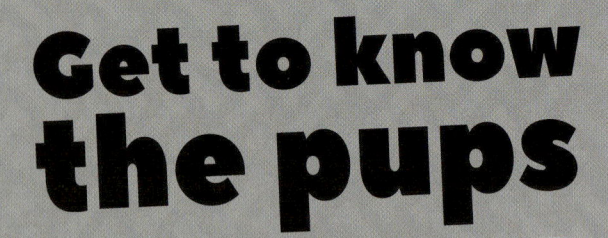

Get to know the pups

Tracker

Tracker is the team's jungle rescue dog. His Pup Pack has a multitool, cables and a grappling hook that he often uses to swing on branches.

Name: Tracker
Breed: Potcake
Skills: Strong sense of hearing and can pick up on tiny sounds. He can also speak Spanish.

Did you know?
Tracker is brave but he doesn't like being in dark places.

Multitool

Cables

50

Jungle rescue

Uh oh! Rubble, Chase and Marshall are lost in the jungle. Help Tracker follow the right path to find his pup pals.

START

FINISH

Can you spot the pup treat? Colour in Tracker's badge when you find it.

Answers on page 75.

51

Meet Tracker

The PAW Patrol's friend Carlos was busy digging for treasure in the jungle.

"I love discovering new things," he said to himself as he worked. "The jungle is a beautiful place, too. I must tell Ryder what a great spot this is."

Ryder was excited to hear about the dig.

"Hey, Carlos! Do you need any help?" he asked over the PupPad.

"No, I'm fine. I'm having a great time," said Carlos. "I'll call you as soon as I find treasure!"

"Okay," laughed Ryder. "We'll be ready to roll when you need us."

As Carlos was chatting he stepped forwards.

"Waaah!" he cried.

He had tumbled into a deep hole, and it was too steep for him to climb out! He had dropped his phone, too, but luckily Ryder had seen everything on his PupPad.

"PAW Patrol, to the PAW Patroller!" Ryder cried. "We've got to rumble to the jungle to save Carlos."

The pups raced aboard their rescue vehicles. But how were they going to find the hole in the jungle and rescue their friend?

Meanwhile, Carlos was trapped and he couldn't reach his phone. "Help! I'm down here," he shouted.

Luckily for Carlos and the PAW Patrol, there was a very special dog in the jungle that day. The pup had big ears that helped him to hear noises from far away. He picked up the sound of Carlos shouting and raced towards him.

The jungle pup soon found the hole.
"My name is Tracker and I'll do whatever it takes to rescue you," he called to Carlos.
"I'm trapped! Can you find my phone and give my friends directions to this hole?" asked Carlos.
"Sí! I'm on it," said Tracker.

Tracker quickly found Carlos's phone. He pressed the screen and it rang through to the PAW Patroller. The pup crew were surprised to see a dog they'd never met before.

"Buenos días. My name is Tracker," he said. "I'll help guide you to the hole where your amigo is trapped."
"Thanks, Tracker. Good to meet you," replied Ryder. "We're on our way."

ssSssssssSsss...

As Tracker was speaking to the PAW Patrol, a dangerous snake was slithering towards the hole. It was the longest, hungriest, meanest snake in the jungle....

"Hey, Señor Slithery. Back off!" Tracker called as he leaped in front of the scary snake.

Down below in the hole, Carlos could hear Tracker barking.

"That's one brave pup," he said.

The snake wasn't scared away for long, but the PAW Patrol arrived just in time to help. They used the PAW Patroller horn to blast out noise that made the reptile slither off for good.

"The PAW Patrol is on a roll!" cried Ryder as they raced towards the hole.

Chase used his night-vision goggles to spot their friend at the bottom of the hole. Then he guided the winch from the back of his vehicle down to Carlos.

"Winch! Retract!" Chase barked, and the winch pulled Carlos up safely.

Finally, Marshall used his X-ray equipment to check that Carlos wasn't hurt.

"I'm fine," he confirmed.

"For being such a brave pup and saving Carlos, we'd like you to join the PAW Patrol, Tracker," said Ryder.

Tracker was given his very own Pup Pack and Pup Tag, with a picture of a tracking compass on it.

"I can't wait to see how this all works," he grinned.

"You look awesome," said Marshall.

Rocky showed Tracker how to use the new Pup Pack before he tried it out.

"Multitool," barked Tracker. Instantly, a robot tool arm slid out from the pack. It had lots of great tools on the end for different jobs.

"Now show everybody your coolest tool," said Ryder.

"Cables!" ordered Tracker.

Zip! Two strong cables with powerful arms slid out of the Pup Pack. Tracker used them to grab a tree branch.

"Now you can swing through the treetops," said Ryder.

"Muchas gracias," cried Tracker – and up he went. "What a great view!"

"Wow. Those cables are swinging!" cheered Rubble.

"Muchas gracias," said Tracker, "I'm all ears and now I'm all gears, too."
"Welcome to the PAW Patrol," said Ryder.
"Get ready to rumble in the jungle with us any time!"

There was one more gift for Tracker as a reward for his bravery. It was a super-cool jeep, just right for jungle adventures.
"A jeep? Just for me?" asked Tracker.
"Sí!" cried the pup crew.

Everest

Everest is the team's mountain rescue pup. Her Pup Pack contains a grappling hook and a folding, rocket-powered snowboard.

Get to know the pups

Name: Everest
Breed: Husky
Skills: Great at sliding down hills on her belly and carrying out snow rescues.

Did you know?
Everest lives on the mountain with Jake and has the bushiest tail out of all the pups!

Pup Pack containing snowboard

Play in the Snow

The pups are playing in the mountains!

Can you find ...

1 owl
2 seals
1 snowman
5 penguins

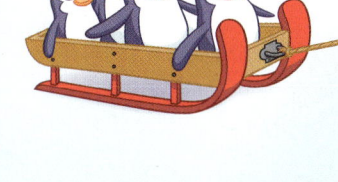

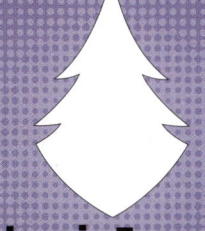

Can you spot the pup treat?

Colour in Everest's badge when you find it.

Answers on page 75.

61

All the apples

Farmer Yumi needs a helping paw or two at harvest time and Rubble and Rocky are just the pups for the job. Which pup will collect the most apples? Count the apples on and around each tree.

Rubble will collect .... apples.

62

Can you spot the pup treat?

Colour in Rubble's badge when you find it.

Rocky will collect .... apples.

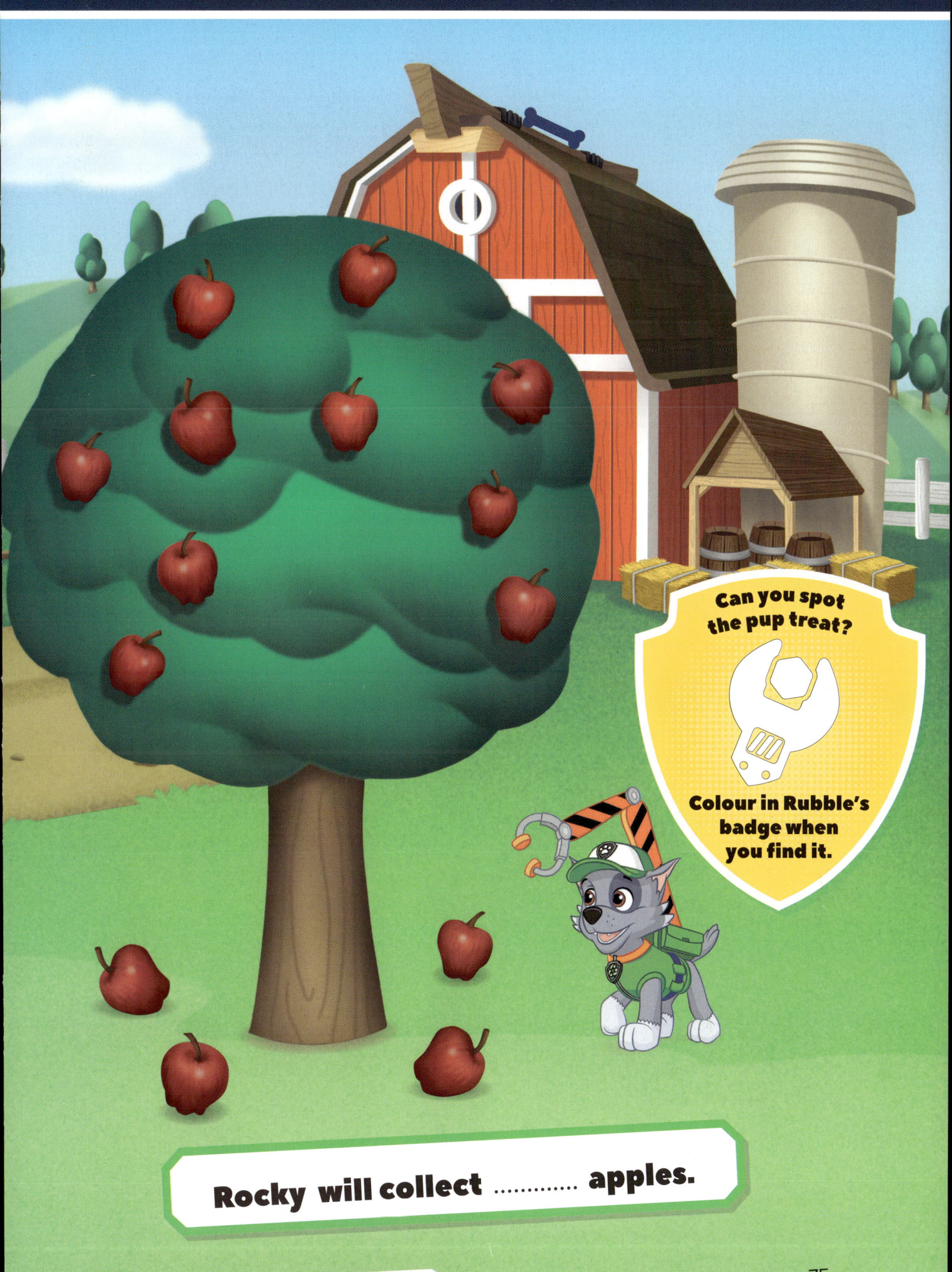

Answers on page 75.

Pups at play

Are you ready for some arty fun? Challenge a pup-loving pal to this PAWsome colouring game!

YOU WILL NEED:

- Two players
- One dice
- Crayons or colouring pencils in dark and light brown, grey, black, blue, yellow, green, orange and pink.

DICE KEY

1 spot	Colour the face
2 spots	Colour an ear
3 spots	Colour the body
4 spots	Colour the tail
5 spots	Colour the collar and tag
6 spots	Colour two legs and paws

WHAT TO DO:

1

Sit with the book turned round so that the picture of Chase is in front of player one and Rocky is in front of player two.

2

Take it in turns to roll the dice. The player with the highest number should go first.

3

Each time you roll the dice, check the **DICE KEY** and colour in the part of the pup that matches the number of spots on the dice.

4

Take it in turns to throw the dice and colour the pictures. The winner is the first player to have a fully coloured pup.

If you throw a number, but you have already coloured that part, pass the dice on and miss a turn.

CHASE
1

2
ROCKY

Ready for action activities

The PAW Patrol is ready to roll! Follow the path and complete the activities along the way.

START

Colour in the orange traffic cones and then trace along the dotted trail without touching the cones.

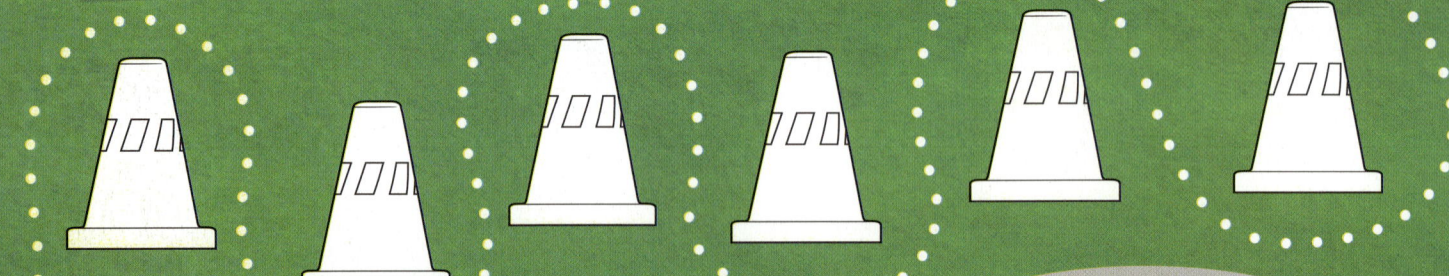

Rocky is recycling. How many plastic bottles can you count?

FINISH

Can you spot the pup treat?

Colour in Everest's badge when you find it.

66

Whizz!

Trace over the letters to help Skye fly high in her helicopter.

Marshall is practising his fire-fighting skills. Draw flames for him to put out with his water cannon.

Rubble is hard at work. Join the dots and then colour in his yellow digger.

Answers on page 76.

67

Fire training trail

Find a friend and join Marshall as he practises his fire pup moves. Who will complete the course first and win the Top Fire Pup badge?

HOW TO PLAY:

1. Using coins for counters, take turns to roll the dice and move around the board the same number of spaces as the number thrown.

2. If you land on an instruction space, do what it says.

3. The first player to reach the finish wins.

START

1 Ruff-ruff ready? START.

2

3

4 Wrong way! Go back 2 spaces.

5

6 You've taken a tumble. Miss a turn.

7

8 Get a lift. Move forward 3 spaces

Can you spot the pup treat?

Colour in Marshall's badge when you find it.

9

10 You've lost your fire hat. Go back 1 space.

11

12 The PAW Patrol cheers you on. Move forward 2 spaces

13

14

15 Pause for a high-paw. Miss a turn.

16

17 You hit the target! Move forward 1 space.

18

19

20 FINISH. Top Fire Pup!

69

Cone crazy

Rubble has set out his cones and he's ready to get digging. See if you can spot the following among the rows of traffic cones:

1. The upside-down cone.
2. The smallest cone.
3. The different coloured cone.

Answers on page 76.

Have you found the pup treat? Colour in Chase's badge when you find it.

Back in the box

Rocky always has the right tools for the job. Help him put them back in the toolbox by drawing lines from each tool to the matching shadow.

Can you spot the pup treat? Colour in Rocky's badge when you find it.

a   b   c   d   e

1   2   3   4   5

Answers on page 76.

71

PAWsome masks

Do you want to join the PAW Patrol and save the day in Adventure Bay?

Ask an adult for help!

1 Remove the mask pages at the back of the book. Stick the pages on thin card and carefully cut them out.

Here's how to make your PAWsome masks:

2 Cut out the eyeholes.

3 Use a pencil to make small holes on either side.

4 Attach elastic through the small holes.

5 Pick a mask and give the rest to your pals.

6 Go and have a pup-tastic adventure together!

Doggy dominoes

Here's how to play a pup-tastic game of Doggy dominoes:

Remove the domino pages at the back of the book. Stick the pages on thin card and cut out the dominoes.

Ask an adult for help!

1 Find a friend to play with.

2 Deal 6 dominoes each and put the rest in a pile.

3 Take it in turns to place a domino in the middle.

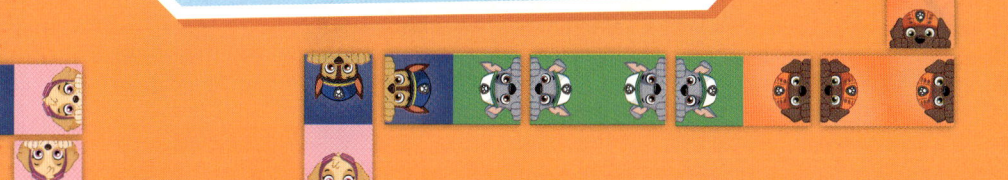

4 The domino the next player places must match one of the ends.

5 If you can't play, pick up a domino from the pile.

6 The winner is the first player to place all of their dominoes.

Answers

Page 9

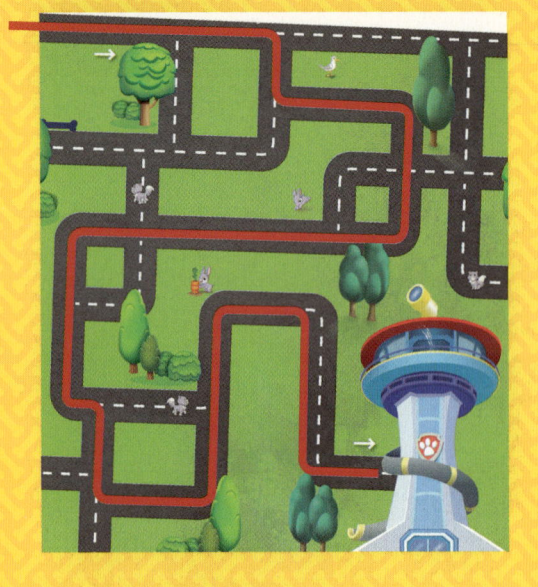

Pages 12-13

Zuma is missing

Page 17

Pages 26-27
1. Chase
2. Pink
3. Marshall
4. Bone
5. Marshall
6. No

Page 29
Rubble C is the different Rubble

Page 30

Page 31

Page 32
1. 5 Marshalls
2. 3 Skyes
3. 5 Zumas
4. 7 Rockys

Page **33**
1b, 2d, 3a, 4c

Page **35**
1c, 2b, 3e, 4a, 5d

Pages **36-37**
Chase is the tallest member of the team
Skye is the smallest member of the team
Rocky and Tracker are wearing green hats
Marshall, Zuma and Rubble are wearing helmets
Everest has got a woolly hat on
Chase is wearing a police hat

Pages **38-39**

Page **41**
1c, 2d, 3b

Pages **42-43**
15 stars

Pages **44-45**
1. CHASE, 2. MARSHALL, 3. ROCKY
4. SKYE, 5. ZUMA, 6. RUBBLE
7. TRACKER, 8. EVEREST

Page **47**
1. 3
2. 3
3. 2

Page **51**

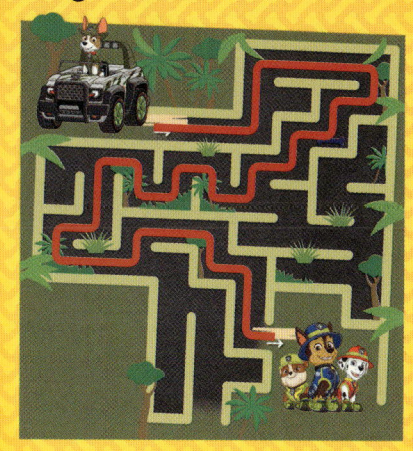

Page **61**

Pages **62-63**
Rubble will collect 16 apples and Rocky will collect 14 apples. Rubble will collect the most apples.

Answers

Pages 66-67
Rocky is recycling 5 plastic bottles.
Rubble - join the dots.

Page 70

Page 71
a4, b1, c5, d2, e3

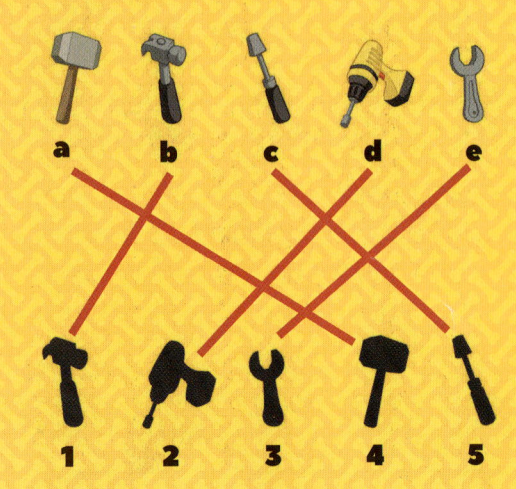

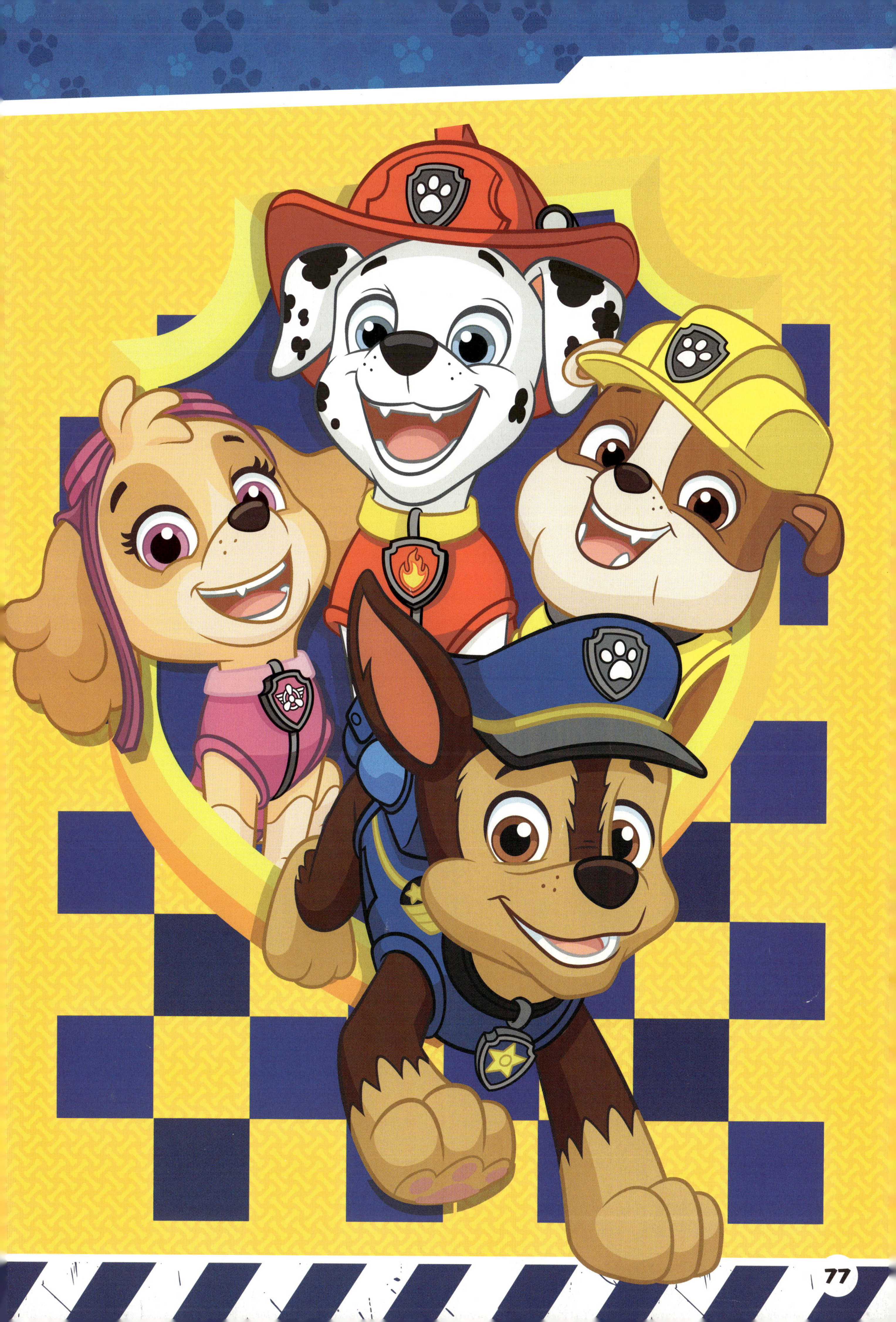

©2018 Spin Master
PAW Productions Inc.

©2018 Spin Master
PAW Productions Inc.

©2018 Spin Master
PAW Productions Inc.

Rubble

Cut out the mask.

Badge
Ask an adult to attach a safety pin.

Cut out the small holes.

Cut out the eyeholes.

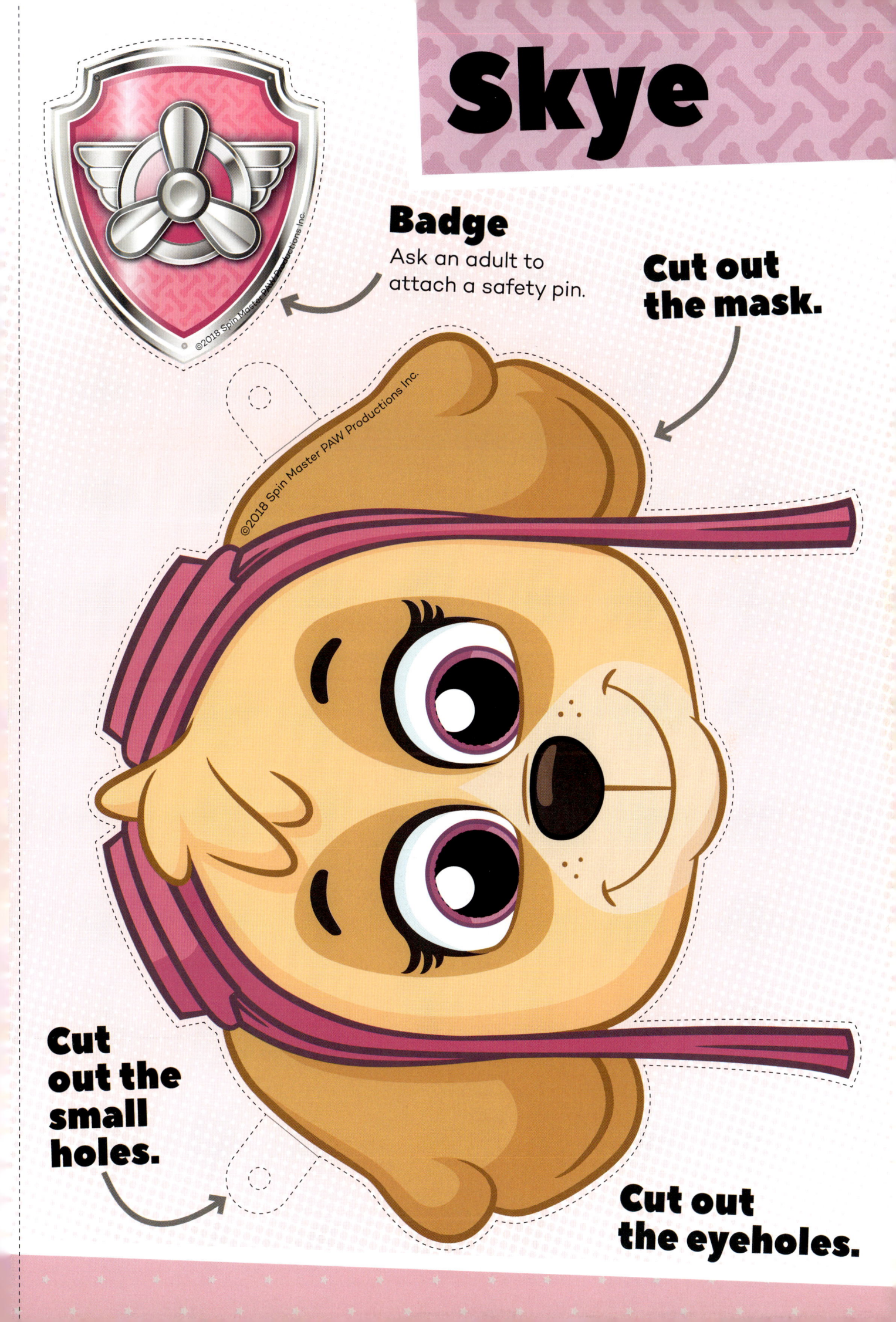

Skye

Badge
Ask an adult to attach a safety pin.

Cut out the mask.

Cut out the small holes.

Cut out the eyeholes.

©2018 Spin Master
PAW Productions Inc.

©2018 Spin Master
PAW Productions Inc.

©2018 Spin Master
PAW Productions Inc.

©2018 Spin Master
PAW Productions Inc.

Chase

Cut out the mask.

Badge
Ask an adult to attach a safety pin.

Cut out the small holes.

Cut out the eyeholes.

Marshall

Badge
Ask an adult to attach a safety pin.

Cut out the mask.

Cut out the small holes.

Cut out the eyeholes.

©2018 Spin Master PAW Productions Inc.

©2018 Spin Master
PAW Productions Inc.

©2018 Spin Master
PAW Productions Inc.

©2018 Spin Master
PAW Productions Inc.

©2018 Spin Master
PAW Productions Inc.

Zuma

Badge
Ask an adult to attach a safety pin.

Cut out the mask.

Cut out the small holes.

Cut out the eyeholes.

Rocky

Badge Ask an adult to attach a safety pin.

Cut out the mask.

Cut out the eyeholes.

Cut out the small holes.

©2018 Spin Master
PAW Productions Inc.

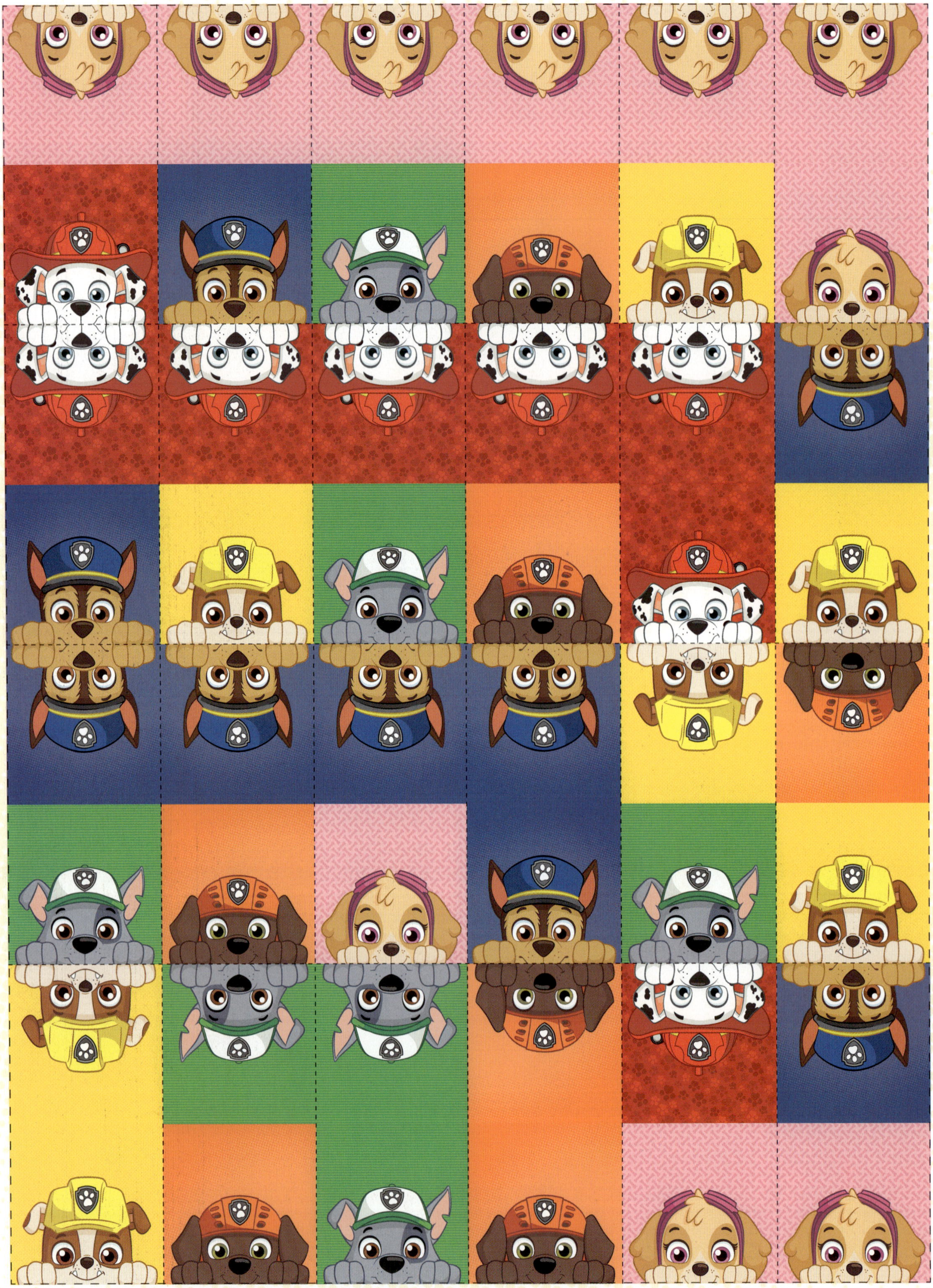

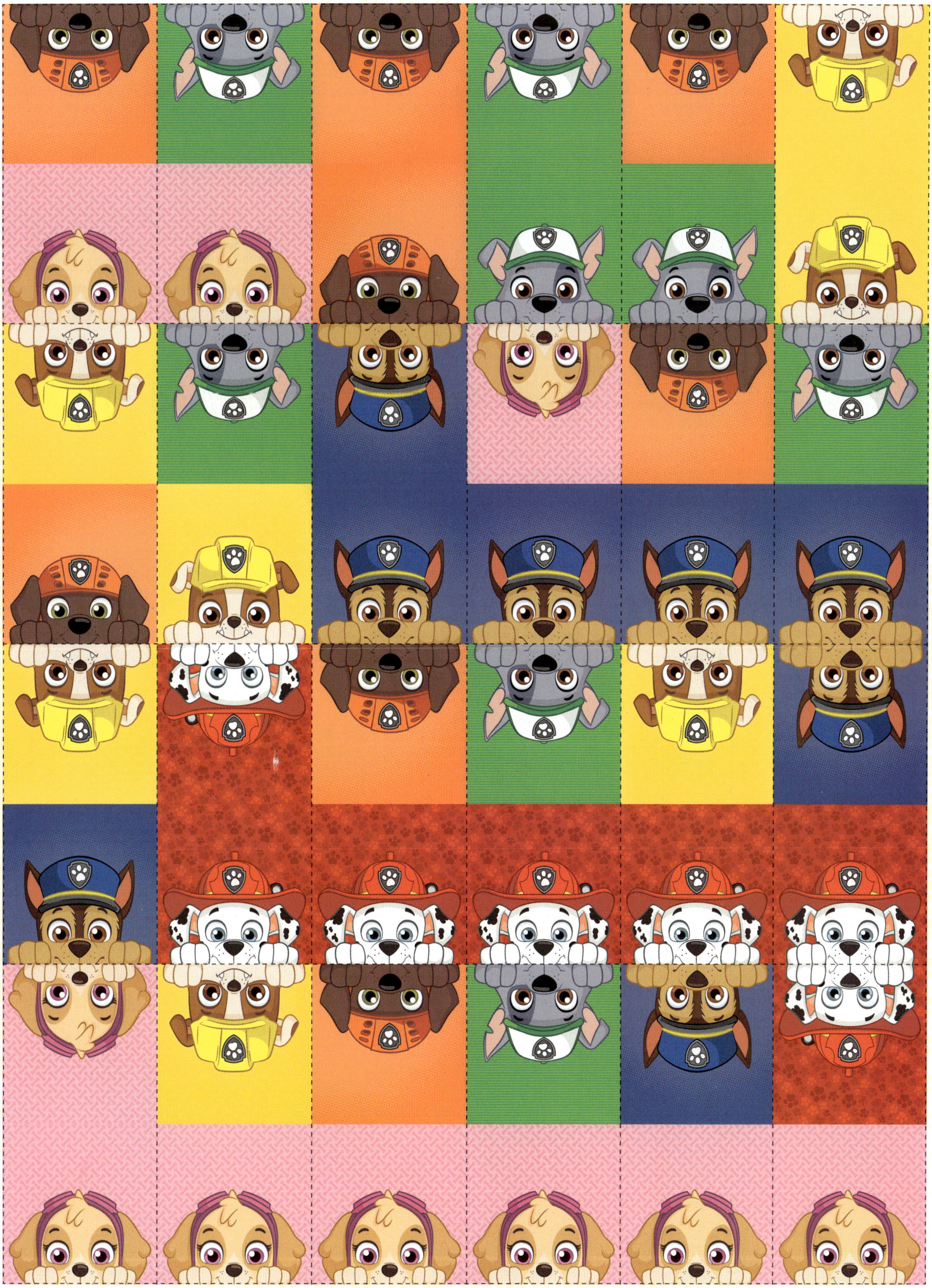